I0008083

UNLOCK THE CODE

---

*The Ultimate Guide to Advancing
from Junior to Senior Software Engineer
in 7 Actionable Steps*

DMYTRO KHMELENKO

DMYTRO KHMELENKO

Editor: Anastasia Mazur

Printed Worldwide
First Printing 2021
First Edition 2021

ISBN 9798526282567

To my family and friends who believe in me, support and inspire me every single day

Присвячується моїй сім'ї і друзям, за віру в мене, підтримку і натхнення щодня

Table of Contents

About the Author

Dmytro is a software engineer with over 10 years of professional experience. He used to develop applications for various mobile platforms and later shifted to building backend systems, falling in love with Ruby on Rails and Python.

Although Dmytro is still 100% engaged in programming, his interests are not only in writing the clean code but also in sharing his knowledge and mentoring other engineers.

The author exercises pragmatism proving every day that practice is the best teacher and judge, and lives with a 'done is better than perfect' attitude (which regularly causes small battles with the clean code preacher in his head). As part of this philosophy, Dmytro is never tired of reminding teams how agile methodologies help launch products fast and why everyone should learn them.

Dmytro is a keen traveler: this particular book was commenced after surfing sessions on the island of Madeira but because holidays don't last forever, he had to finish it surrounded by beige walls in his apartment in Munich. And his next vacation starts only when the last comma is where it belongs in this book. Or maybe not. Otherwise, why would iterations aka book editions exist?

Dmytro also likes doing sports, reading non-fiction books, and discovering new trends in the tech industry. You can reach him on Twitter (@dkhmelenko) where he regularly shares the insights from his daily work.

Introduction

On May 13, 2011 I walked an empty street and arrived at an old red brick building. It had been a factory and now its rooms were rented as offices. Small companies that didn't need luxury places lived here. It was enough to run a business.

I went upstairs and knocked on the door. No reply. It was 8:30 AM, Friday. Not just a Friday — Friday, 13! I went outside and sat down on a bench. I was breathing unevenly, my heart beating like crazy but nobody could see it. It was supposed to be my first working day ever, the launch of my career. I was nervous but also excited.

A few minutes later my colleague Michael arrived. Together we entered a small room, clean and neat. Six desks with computers along the walls. He showed me towards my station. The day has begun.

Later the rest of the colleagues came. Now there were five of us, including me. The manager explained general rules and introduced me to my mentor. Step by step, they guided me through the process.

You can't expect a lot from the first day. It is usually onboarding and no real work happens.

But I felt like a squeezed lemon.

The amount of information was overwhelming. The way we worked and communicated, the software and approaches we used, the projects we had. Everything was new to me and my head was about to blow. Nothing bad happened to me on Friday 13, on the contrary, — yet gigabytes of new information ran over me like a freight train.

Eventually, when the day was over and I arrived home, my family was dying to hear my report: the colleagues, the office, how my working days would look like. Especially because I was invited to join the team so rapidly — only one hour after a job interview on a Thursday evening.

Despite the exhaustion, I patiently described everything in detail. I needed it, too: to reflect on the day full of emotions, surprises and information — my first working day!

Over the years, I moved cities, changed jobs, and met a lot of people. But I still remember that first day.

And I remember a couple of weeks after it.

I still felt a bit lost. Many things I had in mind regarding software development differed a lot. The reality conflicted with what we had learned at the uni in terms of applicability, and many aspects of professional life were missing in university courses. The real work prepared a lot of discoveries.

Every year, I got to know more and more things. Some of them I learned because of the project specifics, while others were more general. And every time something new popped up, I was wondering why nobody told me about it in the university. If it is essential for software engineers, why don't computer science courses cover it?

Unfortunately, even the best universities don't provide the full picture of what awaits students in the future. If they did, trainees and junior developers could catch up with projects faster. They would not feel overwhelmed with concepts, approaches, tools, and many other unknown things.

This is why I decided to write this book. I believe the preparation has to be as real as possible to the industry standards. We need to show proven approaches and methodologies to beginners early and constantly adjust them accordingly.

Eleanor Roosevelt said once: "Learn from the mistakes of others. You can't live long enough to make them all yourself".

In this book, I gathered everything I learned in my 10-years career in the software engineering industry for different types of companies: outsourcing, agency, product. The knowledge shared in this book will help anybody making their first steps as a software developer.

This book is not an autobiography. It is a collection of advice on how to make progress and become a great software engineer. Engineers with little experience will also find it useful. You will learn what else is important to know except programming. Some areas are not related to writing code and yet require your attention. Certain things need exploring and awareness while others are achievable only through practice. Senior developers will find this book helpful as well. It may remind them of all the challenges they went through and learn by reflecting on the experience which sometimes gives unexpected results.

I can't give you a "silver bullet" to become an excellent engineer. However, with all the insights, you will be able to discover your potential and the opportunities around you. This is a guide for the professional path in software development.

Together, we can make the entire industry a bit better.

What is covered in this book

We used to imagine a software engineer as someone staring at a computer for days on end. However, software development is not only about writing code. It is not only about it anymore.

Programming still occupies a large portion of our time but many duties come along.

I find the following areas extremely important for everybody who wants to be a great engineer. These sections explore the following topics:

Technical Stack to Master

This section is dedicated to the hard skills of every software developer. No matter if you work with the front end, mobile, or backend, or doing full-stack development, there are many things in common. Even though we use different frameworks and programming languages, we still build software.

Version control systems, popular data structures, terminal commands are only a few examples every software engineer needs to grasp. We keep using them day-to-day without paying much attention. They are kind of secondary but the lack of knowledge and experience with these tools drags us back on our way to excellence.

In this section, we will go through these common tools and techniques every developer should master sooner.

Product Thinking

Once a software engineer feels confident enough about the framework they use on a daily basis, they come to a point where they can help business grow. This is an important milestone. After this turning point, product development gains momentum and adds points to usability.

However, not every engineer realizes how important product thinking is. This section is dedicated to how every software developer can turn it on. We will explore a few important approaches product teams use proactively. It should intrigue you to start thinking of adopting it in your company.

Collaboration

I wish the need for collaboration should not have been discussed again and again.

But we are not there yet. Every team has people that resist collaborating with others.

They struggle to find touch points. The whole team gets frustrated, and work stops making you happy. Moreover, the company's revenue starts going down.

Curiously, it is possible to fix it — without any technical nitty-gritty.

Learning

Something I understood for myself is that being a good software engineer requires lifelong learning. Technologies develop at a very rapid pace. Once you learn a library or framework, you cannot relax and use it until you retire. Every year new improvements are coming up and we have to adjust our solutions. A good example is Java. When I graduated from the university, everyone was using Java 6. These days, the Java version is 16. If you don't catch up with the recent changes, your value as an engineer goes down.

In this section, we will see how to keep learning and possible directions to grow. We will go through interesting books recognized by many software developers worldwide which I found particularly useful for myself. We will also check various opportunities for personal growth.

Knowledge Sharing

This section talks about why exactly knowledge sharing is important. Over years of work, each of us gets unique experience. We pay for it with time and sweat. Why not share it with others? You can't imagine now how many people would love to hear about your success, failures and learnings! You can get something from it, too.

We will discuss how speaking at conferences and meetups can be beneficial not only for the audience but also for you as a speaker. And not only speaking at conferences — as not everyone is excited about an opportunity to mumble something to an audience of strangers. Other knowledge sharing modes can make you more comfortable and still be beneficial.

Project Management

Some software engineers see the project manager position as a next step in their career. Without discussing its advantages and disadvantages, we will talk about the project lifecycle and your role in it. Understanding how each project grows is important for everyone. Dealing with deadlines and estimations requires special attention as well.

As a software developer, you will see the challenges of the entire project and not only some certain technical complications. The better process understanding, the more precise the goal.

Leadership

In the last section, we will talk about leadership. Good leadership always brings outstanding results. Bad leaders can ruin well-established teams and processes.

It is not an ultimate guide on how to become the leader in everything but rather touching upon a few leadership aspects crucial for IT. It will be a good start for those who want to explore more.

Recommended Resources

In this small section, I gathered all the books and other resources that I am going to mention along the book and that helped me in my career — so that you have them in one place.

Technical Stack to Master

Every developer uses one or several programming languages every day. For people outside of the IT industry, that might sound enough — because what else is needed to be a developer? However, it is not true. In daily work, programmers play with many more tools. They are almost as equally important as programming languages. It can be about systems or specific approaches. Mastering these things helps to push one's career and enables fast and efficient work.

Version Control System

Knowing the history of feature development is important for any product. This is why a version control system (VCS) is a must for any company, especially if more than one person works with code.

VCS enables you to see the history of all changes in code: when a new line of code was added and by whom — to trace back previous changes. If a critical bug gets into the code, reverting those changes becomes an easy task.

At the moment, the most popular system is Git. Invest some time to understand how it works internally. Many tutorials, including the official one, will help you. Learning begins with a simple command and they will be enough for you for a while before you will need to advance.

Many companies use Git every day but it is not the only VCS. Subversion and Mercurial have similar functions but different internals. Understanding the basic principles (such as branch and commit) of any VCS takes handling the source code to the next level.

If programmers had gods, VCS would be one of them — so many hours and sweat it has saved (and more on it in the Learning section about my own mistakes).

It's been such an integral part of my work that I need to think back to my university years to remember life without it. We didn't use Git. Instead, we would have multiple copies of folders and documents. The initial document would be named *task.txt*.

After the professor's feedback, a copy of the file named *task2.txt* would appear. The story would be endless with files named *task3.txt*, *task4.txt* and so on piling in folders. After a while, my professor would ask: "Do you remember the proposal you showed a few weeks ago? I think we should revise it". I had to spend an entire evening trying to figure out which file those changes were. Naturally, I couldn't remember such details. It was a nightmare. And if I had had a proper version control system, I would have been able to scan through the changes in a matter of minutes. I could have compared history snapshots and found the necessary ones.

VCS is an important piece of a software building cycle. Now bare with me. Knowing the basics of Git and being proficient is like night and day. Advanced Git application is jaw-dropping.

For example, deleting all local branches already merged to the master branch.

Over time you can have multiple unrelated branches. Some find it messy and have trouble picking a unique branch name or struggle with the autocomplete feature suggesting to switch to many branches. And you want to keep things clean. Running this command will do magic and remove all merged branches.

git branch --merged | egrep -v "(^*|master)" | xargs git branch -d

What about checking the log? Running a simple log command returns a lot of plain text hard to read. If you ever used a UI tool for work with Git (for example, SourceTree or Tower), you saw the visual representation of the branches' lifecycle — when each of them was created, the commits it had, and when it was merged. It is kind of a tree.

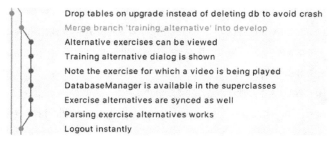

Drop tables on upgrade instead of deleting db to avoid crash
Merge branch 'training_alternative' into develop
Alternative exercises can be viewed
Training alternative dialog is shown
Note the exercise for which a video is being played
DatabaseManager is available in the superclasses
Exercise alternatives are synced as well
Parsing exercise alternatives works
Logout instantly

But what would you say if I told you that it is possible with Git CLI as well? Check out the following command:

*git log --graph --pretty=format:'%Cred%h%Creset -
%C(yellow)%d%Creset %s %Cgreen(%cr) %C(bold
blue)<%an>%Creset' --abbrev-commit*

```
| \ \
| * | c99cd005 - add refresh_token spec (1 year, 3 months ago)
| * | dec28bf3 - add audience to refresh tokens (1 year, 3 mon
| * | 33222b89 - delete refresh tokens if forget password (1 y
| * | 0322161e - Use freezed strings for audience (1 year, 3 m
| * | 408440d5 - client can refresh restricted tokens (1 year,
| |/
```

These commands look complex but they make your life easier. You can avoid typing them every time by creating an alias.

I learned these tricks from Roger, a colleague of mine. Although he admitted Git worked magic, he saw no mystery: he knew and could explain in detail what happened under Git's hood.

Those days, he gave several internal Git workshops, and I will describe one of them. A few days before the workshop, he asked for my permission to use my name in his presentation. I was curious and agreed.

During the presentation, to the audience's awe, he changed the user name and user email is Git configuration. Now every commit he did it looked like mine. He demonstrated how easy it was to fake user identity in Git. "It's impossible," the audience said, but it was true. If Roger was completely evil, he could create malicious pull requests or simply add commits to existing pull requests under my name and set me up big times.

Thankfully, the next thing he showed was preventing such mishaps.

The solution is called *signed commits*. If you see this, it means the commits from my name are trustful. Moreover, it is possible to force having only signed commits in the repository. This relatively simple thing can bring your code a lot of security.

The take-away: Git is a powerful tool, and investing some time to learn Git internals and documentation is worth it. Over the years, I still find curious things such as various arguments to command and their impact.

One of my colleagues even said that version control systems should be used more proactively. And not only in software development. Many processes would benefit from it, like copywriting or legislation. And I agree with him.

Continuous Integration & Continuous Delivery

The concept of continuous integration (CI) and continuous delivery (CD) is actively used in the software engineering industry. While not being rocket science, they enable building reliable software.

Continuous integration is a common practice when the code gets integrated sooner. Every team member or a single developer brings their piece of code to the shared place in a short period of time. For example, instead of developing a feature independently for a year, small parts of it get merged frequently, even on a daily basis.

In this case, the integration is simpler. Unit and integration tests for all components guarantees nothing gets broken when everybody merges their code. Otherwise, for a long-running feature development merging the changes will result in a lot of conflicts. Believe me, you don't want to spend hours resolving a pile of problems when you can do it smoothly day by day.

Continuous delivery has a similar approach. The solution you are building gets delivered frequently. Whenever a new feature merges to the main branch of the repository, you want to give it to testers or beta users. Continuous delivery utilizes a mechanism to assemble and distribute the testable product. This enables the engineering team to receive feedback and fix bugs earlier.

There are many available services for CI and CD, running in the cloud or on-prem.

The important thing is to understand how to build a pipeline — the sequence of actions to be performed. It can be syntactic code analysis, unit tests, integration tests, assembling and binaries. The pipeline can be different depending on the technology stack but the concept stays the same. Setting the pipeline is what matters.

The next level is to optimize the setup according to the project needs and make it efficient. Identifying the slowest job, giving priority to certain jobs, performance jobs in parallel when possible — these are a few examples of pipeline optimization. Apart from reducing costs, it leads to increasing the developer's happiness. Imagine, every developer has to wait 30 minutes before merging a pull request. Then fixing a typo would lead to another 30 minutes of waiting. Caching the previous job results and reusing them could reduce the build time from 30 min to 5 min.

CI/CD doesn't require a college course. However, unless you try building it at least once, understanding what people talk about would be hard.

The benefits of CI/CD are clear. Everybody wants to be sure that with every newly added line of code nothing gets broken — as it often happens in big systems. While CI is your safety net, CD helps you to deliver solutions as fast as possible. The user base gets adapted slowly to every change in a product rather than to a 100 features-release once a month. CI/CD benefits users and takes care of developers' time and nerve cells — therefore it deserves mastering!

Automation

I know a few developers who tend to write a script for everything. Any action that others perform manually is seen as an opportunity to automate. I can't tell you how much I enjoy hearing their ideas on what could be automated.

Automation is about time-saving but not only. Imagine, a manual action which takes only 5 minutes a day will result in 25 minutes a week or almost 2 hours a month. That doesn't seem like too much time. But automating it will take the load off your shoulders — you won't need to remember doing the task and can concentrate on more pleasant things.

Let's be honest: each of us had those days when we realized we had forgotten to perform some routine action the day before. Like preparing a report or uploading a log file to the server. Automating that action brings confidence that the action is performed — and exactly when it's needed.

Besides, humans make mistakes — big or small, even with small and repeated tasks. Like trying to download a file without being logged into the system. That would take more time: sign in and try again. Automation helps to avoid it. Defined actions are executed in a certain sequence. This is the beauty of it — when the script is in its place.

When I was doing mobile development, we did an app release every two weeks. The release included a sequence of actions such as reading the release branch in Git, bumping up the app version, assembling the binaries, and uploading them to the marketplace. All together, it took about 20 minutes. The task was assigned to a dedicated engineer. The engineer was trained to release fast and efficiently. However, when he was sick or on vacation someone else had to pick up the release process. Since not everybody was aware of the current release process, the release wasn't done properly. That was our bottleneck. After a while, we came to the conclusion that the entire process could be automated. Slowly, iteration by iteration we achieved the goal. All release processes turned into a one-click action. Every developer (and even non-developers) could do an app release. Everything was behind the scenes. A bunch of scripts were working for us. We had a guarantee that the release was done properly and the steps were executed in a defined order. No more dependency on a single person.

Here's another example of how automation saved me a few minutes every day. The team was building an application with lots of pictures and visuals. Every time my teammates added new images to the application, I had to remind them to optimize the image size so that the installation file wouldn't take too much disk space. They knew the images had to be optimized but often forgot to do it. Babysitting this process wasn't the best investment of my time so I came up with a script that checked if the visual assets satisfied the requirements. It ran every time a developer created a pull request. If the size of the newly added pictures went over the threshold, the developer received a notification. In the end, the few lines long script helped many people: I stopped watching all newly added assets, my teammates received an automated reminder, and the application stopped growing in size.

However, one of the most striking examples from my professional life of how automation makes a developer's work easier is about localizing applications which we always had to do. Sometimes it was two-three languages and sometimes more than ten. That was not a simple task. Just imagine translators returning the list of all strings for every language. Besides, using a certain format for translation copies in the app turned things even more complex.

In an ideal world, the following would happen: the app is ready, what was planned is implemented, all strings are provided to translators and later you take those strings and apply. Done. Everything is completed, the app supports many languages.

Everybody is happy, a big celebration is organized on the roof terrace, the project is over and nobody goes back to it.

Unfortunately, the world is not like that. What usually happens is the following: localization starts too early when the application is still in active development. Some strings need to be changed over time. New strings must be added or new language must be supported. Just think about it: every small action regarding localization involves developer's work. What if each of those actions happens every day or a few times per day? Every translator works independently and can respond with fresh localized strings once they are ready. Every request from a translator should be processed without being lost. This process not only requires too much manual work for software engineers, it needs to be synchronous!

Naturally, this case cries for automation.

Thankfully, our colleague Martin tried to automate everything around him. And this task felt like a challenge.

Martin discovered that the localization tool the translators used had an API. He implemented a script that pulled all the localizations from that API. Then they were converted to a specific format, XML for the Android operating system. The script ran and put all translations to XML files. Then another script took all those XML files and created a pull request to the repository with the application source code.

Voila: now instead of all that manual work, an automatic job ran every day and created a pull request to the repository. Developers needed only to make sure nothing was wrong and merge it.

But Martin went even further. What was the reason to check this pull request if the team had continuous integration in place which already did checks and could guarantee the code was not broken? Since all changes to the code had to be done only through pull requests, Martin implemented another bot. It received a callback when localization automatically submitted a review and merged it to the main branch. This was a genius solution.

Remember how many actions engineers need to perform in order to integrate new translations to the app? Now they don't have to do any. The process was completely automated and error-proof. New localized strings were constantly delivered to the app with zero work from the engineering side. If this can't convince you how automating certain things speed up the development process and save time, I don't know what can.

Many script languages are available: Bash, Powershell, Python are most used nowadays. Each of them has its own advantages and disadvantages. My favourite is Python, with many capabilities and ease of use. Try playing around with each of them, check if it meets your needs. And master at least one of them. Once you know the language capabilities, you will see the things that can be automated.

Finally, having the skill to identify actions that can be automated proves the seniority of an engineer.

Integrated Development Environment (IDE)

Some developers have "holy wars" discussing which IDE is the best. So important it is.

Integrated development environment is similar to regular text editors in the way that you can write code in both. However, this is the only thing in common. IDE has specific tools for programming: build automation tools and a debugger integrated, etc.

Various IDEs offer different features. Sticking to one is a matter of personal preference.

Why is it important to be good at IDE? Firstly, it is the question of efficiency. Debugging, refactoring, and navigation through the code are the most used actions in every IDE. Can you imagine renaming a function used in 100 places? Or finding all places where a certain class is being used? Or how to enable breakpoint only when the variable is set to 'true'?

Most IDEs offer a lot of great features. Some of them might not be used that often, others are so common nobody can imagine working without them.

Mastering work in IDE can be compared to a knife. Everybody knows this tool is for cutting things. But you can also do wood carving if you are good at it. Beginners see IDE as a text editor with multiple toolbars. Not impressive. Professionals though can achieve fast and outstanding results — they know how the tool works and what is possible.

Investing some time to explore features of the IDE is worth it. Whole discussion panels at conferences are dedicated to exploring IDE capabilities with advanced users.

Here are only a few examples what IDE can offer:

- Find all usages of variable, function or class;

- Refactor function name and signature;

- Debugging (using breakpoints, conditional breakpoints, logging);

- Application performance analysis (e.g. memory usage to find memory leaks, execution duration);

- Integrated version control system;

- Navigate between files, directories, sub-projects, modules, dependencies and other logical parts of the project.

As you see, the list is impressive. A developer who knows and uses it extensively shows a great performance.

Lastly, no matter which IDE you stick to, no matter what others say about your choice, keep on practicing. What matters is being confident with the tool. I've seen engineers using simple text editors with a bunch of plugins and producing stunning things. It is all about how good you are with the tools you have.

Design Patterns

Once a person learns how to code, the confidence level increases. All problems seem to be solvable. But it might be misleading.

"I suppose it is tempting, if the only tool you have is a hammer, to treat everything as if it were a nail."

- Abraham Maslow

Applying design patterns is a powerful approach in the software industry nowadays. Spend some time to master at least a few most popular patterns. For example, *Observer, Factory, Singleton, Facade*. In fact, there are many of them. With a proper application of design patterns, final solutions become solid and scalable. Maintaining the code gets easier. As many patterns are recognizable by developers, it helps others to navigate through the code faster and extend it.

In one company, we had a tradition. Every Thursday afternoon, we would gather in front of the whiteboard and try to solve various challenges. We discussed architecture ideas and specific issues we'd had in recent weeks. That was a great format to improve ourselves and deal with real-world problems.

One of our discussions revolved around design patterns. We were arguing which design patterns are used more often so that students in universities could dedicate more time to them. During that discussion, an Observer pattern caught our attention and we realized how widely this pattern is used. The entire asynchronous and reactive programming paradigms are based on the Observer pattern. Its obvious value prompted us to include it in the must-learn list.

Then we asked ourselves the following: If I were a professor at university, how would I explain the Observer pattern to my students? It should be clear, straightforward and applicable. The brainstorming process helped us to review the pattern's implementation and its proper application. I still remember many variations of the Observer pattern's implementation.

Go ahead and pick up a similar topic to discuss with the engineers in your team. You will be surprised by how much you can learn from each other. It will teach you to express your thoughts in a manner that leaves no questions. In some cases, that can motivate you to revise the materials from the past and look at them from another perspective.

To get a hang of it, read *Design Patterns* by the "Gang of Four". The book describes many different patterns and situations to apply them. Every developer must read it.

Improve Programming Skills

Completing a programming course is never enough. To succeed as a developer, you have to continue programming all the time — sometimes more, sometimes less, but consistently.

You might be wondering why, because as a software engineer, you have many coding challenges. Unfortunately, this is usually not true. Developers indeed have challenging tasks, design complex architectures, and solve unique issues. But not every day. Probably not even every month.

These days many things are encapsulated well within existing libraries. For example, building an image recognition application doesn't require a master's degree in mathematics anymore. Life's become simpler for everybody. An experienced software engineer can build products using various frameworks. They end up dealing with frameworks and resolving business needs. While the product 100% benefits from it, engineers can start losing skills in solving technical problems.

I will not bother you with the discussion whether knowing how to rebalance a binary tree is essential to the majority of software developer jobs. But understanding the problem and being able to solve it can be insightful for many other daily tasks. This is exactly what those kinds of tasks are teaching us.

Resources such as *HackerRank*, *LeetCode*, and many others can assist with improving your programming skills. Occasionally dedicate an hour to the learning and in one year you will see a huge difference.

Master Data Structures

In computer science courses, we learn many data structures. It all starts with how data is organized and saved on machines. Then we discover more complex structures such as graphs. Some specializations even offer an entire course about graph theory.

The variety of data structures shows how many potential issues are out there. Luckily, the majority of engineering tasks can be resolved only with a few types of data structures. That is, unless you are building a new database engine, a navigation system, or software for a spaceship.

Applying them efficiently will enable your solution's great performance. And from my experience, this is something that is regularly checked during technical interviews for software development positions.

List

The first essential data structure is a list. With the list you can solve many tasks: collect items, loop through them, sort, pass as a parameter, and many more. This data structure is more advanced than a simple array. It offers additional methods for convenient work. Some of those are *remove()*, *indexOf()*, *contains()*.

In different languages, the list is backed by a different internal implementation. In some cases, internally it is implemented with an array, in other cases with a linked list. Here, you need to know the difference as it affects efficiency. For example, an array list has access time O(1) and a linked list has O(n). On the other hand, an array list requires more time to extend space when more and more items get inserted. If the main purpose is to access items, consider an array list. If you are going to mostly add new items, a linked list is a better option.

```kotlin
val names = listOf("Anna", "Sandra", "Maria", "Laura")
val isLauraPresent = names.contains("Beatrice")
```

In the example in Kotlin above, we have a list of female names and then we use the method *contains()* to check if the name Beatrice is in the list. There is nothing wrong with this method, however one thing you have to keep in mind. This method has time complexity O(n). On large lists calling the method *contains()* will cause performance issues. What would you do instead? Check the next structure.

Set

Set is a data structure that guarantees the uniqueness of each element. Internally it uses the concept of Hash Table. For every element, a corresponding hash value is calculated that acts as a key. Implementation can vary depending on the platform.

But nevertheless, the idea remains the same: Set will contain only unique elements with no particular order.

Therefore, every time you have a task to ignore duplicate elements, remember about sets. Usually, it is possible to convert a list to a set. Let's see how it looks in Kotlin.

```
val names = listOf("Lara", "Ben", "Mary", "Ben", "Lucia",
                   "Lara")
val uniqueNames = names.toSet()
```

The set *uniqueNames* will contain only [Lara, Ben, Mary, Lucia]. This is the fastest way to remove duplicates.

Another important property of the set is how it accesses elements. As it is using a hash to retrieve values, the time complexity will be in this case O(1). The same relates to the *contains()* method. It doesn't loop through all elements. That makes time complexity for this method O(1). Keep that in mind if you want to make optimization.

Since Set is a concept from mathematics, performing operations like union, intersection, or a subset on it is easier.

```
val classRoom1 = setOf("Anna", "Ben", "Lara")
val classRoom2 = setOf("Clarice", "Ben", "Patrick")

val intersection = classRoom1.intersect(classRoom2)
```

In the example above in Kotlin, we can see how to quickly find names that are present in both sets using sets intersection.

Dictionary

Dictionary is another powerful data structure in computer science. Every element in a dictionary is represented by a key and a value. There are multiple implementations of dictionaries and every platform has its own specifics. The main feature of dictionaries is to have a specific key for every element.

In a dictionary, the key should stay unique. It acts as a hash in set. Otherwise, it leads to collisions.

```
val capitals = hashMapOf("Berlin" to "Germany",
                         "London" to "UK")
```

This is a classical example of a dictionary where the city is the key and the country is the value. It gives an idea of what a dictionary is. If we add a new item with the same key, it will override an existing item.

Where else would you use a dictionary?

One of the typical use cases is to calculate occurrences of every element in a collection. An item will be a key in a dictionary because it should be unique. The value is the number of occurrences.

Let's look at the example below that calculates the number of occurrences of every character in a string.

```
val input = "I want to be a better programmer"
val dictionary = mutableMapOf<Char, Int>()
for (character in input) {
  dictionary.putIfAbsent(character, 0)
  dictionary[character] = dictionary[character]!! + 1
}
```

A key is a character and the value is how many times this character appeared in the input string. After running this piece in Kotlin, the dictionary will contain the following:

```
{'I'=1, ' '=6, 'w'=1, 'a'=3, 'n'=1, 't'=4, 'o'=2, 'b'=2,
'e'=4, 'r'=4, 'p'=1, 'g'=1, 'm'=2}
```

This is the idea of a dictionary application. The value represents some variable that is associated with a defined key.

***

The world of computer science contains a lot of data structures. Each of them serves its own needs. Some of them are applied widely, others are used only to achieve a very specific goal. If you invest some time in using the data structures from the above, it will be enough to work efficiently with everyday tasks and expand your skills further.

Demonstrate your knowledge about data structures in your next coding interview and increase your chances to get that job!

Functional Programming

Functional programming is not a new paradigm. According to Wikipedia, the idea started popping up in the 1930s. The main concept behind it is to compose functions in a chain.

Unlike the imperative way of programming where developers have to store the state, functional programming is stateless. All computations and data manipulations happen in functions without keeping the intermediate state of the data. You can think of it as a pipe: each piece is a function that receives some data and returns the result. That result becomes an input for another function.

The functional programming concept is powerful and has received the attention of many developers. Many modern programming languages support it.

But what makes this paradigm that favorable? If it only has advantages, why hasn't it replaced the imperative paradigm yet?

The Advantages

Functional programming gets its traction in filtering data and changing the format. If solutions require filtering out some data, changing the order, or picking only certain pieces of data, there is a good chance you are on the right path. Let's explore the following example:

```
city_companies = {
    apple: ["Boston", "Seattle", "San Francisco"],
    uniliver: ["London", "Sussex"],
    microsoft: ["Seattle", "Austin", "Denver"],
    amazon: ["Portland", "Denver", "Washington"],
    starbucks: ["Beijing", "Seattle", "Munich"]
}

tech_giants = [:apple, :microsoft, :amazon]
tech_giants_cities = city_companies
  .select {|company, cities|tech_giants.include?(company)}
  .map {|company, cities| cities}
  .flatten
  .uniq
```

We have a hash where companies are keys and cities are values. We would like to get the cities where tech giants like Apple, Microsoft, and Amazon are located. For that purpose, we filter the hash to select only the tech giants. Then we fetch the cities and remove any duplicates.

The best part of functional programming — it makes code simple and readable. We get our result in only five lines of code.

How much code would it take with an imperative approach?

We would need to have a loop through all the items. In that loop, we would have to use an if statement to check that a certain item is a proper fit. Along with all of that, we would introduce a few temporary variables to save the intermediate state. When you implement it, you have more than five lines of code.

Writing code in a functional way can be addictive as it simplifies many things. This concept has gained popularity in recent years. Many modern languages like Kotlin, Ruby, and Swift use it extensively.

Where to Pay Attention

Along with simple functions like filter and map, there are advanced functions. Attention: chaining these into a long sequence can reduce the code readability in some cases. At that point, the benefit of compact code becomes a problem.

```
total_duration = events.pluck(:duration).compact.sum.round
```

In the example above, chaining together four different functions is not difficult, but you have to know what each function does. Without it, debugging this line can take some time.

This example is in Ruby: it picks the duration attribute from the collection of events. The compact function removes all nullable items. The sum and round functions are simpler: they calculate the sum of the duration and round the final result to the nearest integer.

Every programming language introduces specific functions for processing data structures: *reduce()*, *collect()*, and *fold()* to name a few. In combination with other functions, that can create confusion. Imagine chaining together over ten functions, including advanced ones. I doubt your teammates would be happy dealing with that code. Selecting necessary functions carefully saves a lot of time for you and your team.

You must remember one more thing: the order of functions is important as well. If you have to do filtering and mapping on an array, filtering (if possible) should be done first, and another operation after, because that next operation will be processing an already-reduced dataset.

```
scores = [2.1, 4.2, 6.4, 1.3, 5.6, 7.1, 2.3]

# sorting 3 elements
scores.select{|score| score > 5.0}.sort

# sorting 7 elements
scores.sort.select{|score| score > 5.0}
```

When operations are in the opposite order, it wastes computational resources for processing data that will be excluded later. In the second example, the sorting operation is performed on seven elements. In the first example, it is performed on only three elements. Obviously, the difference in performance will be visible on bigger datasets.

Functional programming is not a magic solution. Software engineers cannot start writing complex systems by solely following that paradigm. It all comes down to your needs. If your application is supposed to be stateless, functional programming is the way to go. However, if your solution is stateful and requires state management, applying a functional approach will look unnatural.

Think of functional programming as another great tool for solving specific problems. Picking up the right instrument to achieve your goal is an important skill — and the functional concept is one of them.

Linux Commands

Every software developer has to know how to use *Bash* commands. In certain situations, a nice user interface may not be available and the only remaining thing is a command line. Running commands through a command line can be even faster than through some graphical interface.

Bash is a powerful tool in Unix systems. Through the terminal commands, it allows performing many actions, in some cases with a root user's rights. What else makes Bash so attractive and popular is the ability to write scripts and organize some flows. Running commands sequentially and repetitively reduces errors significantly and saves a lot of engineering time.

Below you can find a list of the most recognized everyday Bash commands that could simplify your work.

1. ls

ls lists the content in the current directory or passes the directory as a parameter to inspect it.

2. cd

cd stands for change directory. Pass the directory as an argument, and the current directory will be changed to the one you provided. For example, the command *cd /private/Applications* will change the current directory to */private/Applications*.

3. mkdir

mkdir is for creating a new directory (folder). The name of the directory should be provided after this command.

4. cp

cp copies a file from one directory to another. The first parameter is a source file, the second parameter is a destination file.

The usage example will look like this: *cp readme.txt private/readme.txt*. This will copy the file *readme.txt* to the directory */private* and will keep the same file name, *readme.txt*.

5. mv

mv moves files from one directory to another. It has a similar syntax to the *cp* command where we need to provide source and destination files.

6. rm

rm removes a specified file. This command can be used for removing the directory as well but with an additional parameter, -*r*. For example, the command *rm -r /private* will delete the directory */private* and all files in it.

7. cat

cat is an abbreviation of concatenate. This is a standard tool in Unix for reading and writing files.

To read the file *readme.txt*, we need to write *cat readme.txt*, and the content of the file will be shown. To write to the file, use the command *cat > readme.txt*. The file will be overwritten or a new file created if it didn't exist.

To append text to the file, use the command *cat >> readme.txt*. The difference here is in the > and >> operators only. The > redirects the output to the new file or overwrites the existing one, while the >> redirects the output to the new file or appends it to the existing one.

8. grep

grep is another tool in Unix systems. It is designed for simple text search in files or input streams. It has many parameters that can enable a search through multiple files with regular expressions.

The simplest usage of it would be *grep 'hello' readme.txt*, which looks for the word hello in the file *readme.txt*.

9. xargs

xargs works best together with other commands. It takes the input and executes the command, supplying it with the parameter from the input. The simplest example would be *echo "new_dir" | xargs mkdir*. The text *new_dir* is passed as an input to the *xargs* command. Then the command *mkdir new_dir* will be executed and a new directory, *new_dir*, will be created. The connection is made through the pipe operator, |. This operator passes the output of one command to the following command as an input.

10. chmod

chmod changes the permission of the given file. In Unix systems, the file can have read, write, and execute permissions. With this command, it is possible to set the required permission for a file. For example, *chmod +w readme.txt* gives write permission to the file *readme.txt* and *chmod -w readme.txt* removes it.

11. export

export lists all environment variables and sets up a new variable. If no parameters are provided, it will show all environment variables. For example,

export JAVA_HOME=/Applications/jre/jdk

will set up an environment variable *JAVA_HOME* for the current Bash session. If we need to have the variable permanently for all sessions, then we need to put this command to the initialization file (for Bash, it is *~/.bashrc*).

12. ping

ping is a simple command for checking if a remote resource is reachable. For instance, run *ping google.com* to see if the website *google.com* can accept requests and respond to them.

13. curl

curl is another great tool. It is being used for making requests via various protocols to a server. It is known for making requests via the HTTP(-S) protocol to the REST API. A simplest example would be *curl https://www.google.com*. It will return the HTML response of the website. This utility was designed for transferring data, and therefore, it has all the capabilities for that. Setting custom headers, submitting form data, streaming data are only a few to mention.

***

This is not an exhaustive list of all Unix commands. Every developer decides for themselves which Bash commands are very important and which are less so. It depends on tasks and habits. Additionally, each of the commands has multiple parameters that can affect behavior significantly. The best way to explore every command in depth is to run it with the parameter *--help*. This will return a description of the command along with all possible parameters.

Learning Bash commands and applying them daily can boost engineering productivity. They are meant to work in a simple way.

But along with great opportunities comes responsibility. Be careful, as they can be as harmful as they are useful.

Product Thinking

I've worked for various types of companies with various products. Outsourcing, when the product for the client was the source code. Working for an agency building applications and providing clients with products ready to use. Working for a company which has its own product with a big user base.

In the end, the product is what matters. I gathered some observations which can help engineers contribute to better product development.

Listen to Your Users

This advice may seem obvious but is often overlooked, even by experienced teams. Your users can show some pain points which you might never have considered. They can do it via feedback forms or public review platforms. Make sure you dedicate some time regularly to collect the suggestions and analyze how to proceed on them.

Nowadays I try to involve more users in product development.

Don't hesitate to contact a person who provided detailed feedback and get even more details if you can. This will help you understand real user needs. Engineers do not write code for the sake of doing it but to make a product better. When I saw the way people use our product and where they struggle, it lit a bulb inside my brain to make a proposal for a different solution.

At the same time, remember: you can't make every user's wish come true. Henry Ford said: "If I had asked people what they wanted, they would have said faster horses". Customers sometimes don't know what they really want. Use the feedback as an inspiration.

Ask yourself, why you are doing it. Simon Sinek wrote a great book *Start With Why* in which he explains the principles of solving issues effectively and teaches how to integrate those into your team's work.

User Experience

User experience (UX) is essential for any kind of a product you build. It doesn't matter if we are talking about software or a physical product.

Most of the products we use daily don't require user manuals. Products have those, but not everyone reads them.

A product with good UX does not need a manual. And some products can't be helped even with it.

As software engineers, we need to think in terms of what is best for the end-user. Knowing some design principles on different platforms and in collaboration with designers and user researchers, we can build a great experience — clear and simple product usage.

I would recommend reading the book *The Design of Everyday Things* by Don Norman. This book teaches design thinking and gives examples of good and bad design. Honestly, product design is not an easy task. Good things require time, effort and experience.

Tracking Matters

Tracking is essential for product growth. How do you know if a feature you implemented is successful? How many users are using it, how much time, how they are interacting with it and many other hows.

These questions are a headache firstly for product managers. However, as a software engineer, you can help to grow the product. Suggest tracking interactions like scrolling, swiping, using different screens and modal dialogs. Also, don't forget to add the tracking of exceptional situations — for example, lost connection while uploading a picture.

Increase in purchases after improving the onboarding flow

The chart above shows an increase in purchases after we made a couple of improvements in the user onboarding flow. Which of those improvements led to better performance?

Business intelligence teams usually define a set of important metrics for every application. For example, the conversion rate — the share of users who converted from non-paying to paying ones.

Remember the Pareto principle? 80% of the results are built with 20% of the effort. But how can we know what exactly the 20% was? Was it the copies update or the paywall? Or was it a push notification to open the app? With tracking in your app, reproducing customer's behaviors and understanding the impact of every change becomes possible.

Once we were developing a mobile application which provided personalized cooking recipes. There was a free version and a paid one where users had daily menus generated individually. One day we decided to experiment and enabled free access to five breakfast options out of the collection of 50. We were aiming at increasing the engagement which could lead to a higher conversion rate.

Back in those days, our users would cook approximately 1,000 meals per day. If making 5 breakfasts free had given a 2% increase in the number of cooked meals, we would have been happy.

We didn't expect what came next.

On average, the increase was 15%. The engagement skyrocketed. More and more people were using that free content.

The way we discovered that was by adding tracking. Every time a user selected a meal to cook, the application would store the boolean value if the recipe belongs to the list of those defined 5 free breakfasts. Business analysts used this piece of information to make conclusions. Besides, those days more features were delivered, so without tracking, we would not have been able to know why more people started cooking.

As we see, a simple boolean value can make a difference for the business.

This result gave my team an impulse to think about new improvements. The discovery started raising more and more questions. Did it happen because the content was free? Or because it was good? Responding to the questions was our next step but the importance of tracing was never forgotten since then.

Tracking matters but what about its technical side?

First, pick a proper framework/tools for tracking — for example like *Firebase* or *Mixpanel*. Second, check the delay before the data appears on the dashboard and how crucial it is for you. Some businesses need near real-time data, others tolerate a several hours delay.

Lastly, don't forget about unit tests for tracking functionality (having good test coverage is good anyway) — you don't want missing or misleading data. And prepare yourself for great discoveries — because they will surely come.

Fast Prototyping

If you want to see tears on a developer's face, ask them to quickly build a prototype.

Engineers need to invest time building solutions with clean code, do it thoughtfully following best practices, and with good test coverage. Therefore, a bit of our engineering soul dies silently when we are asked to do it in a hurry. As much as I hate it though, fast prototyping is crucial for thriving developers.

Once my team agreed to build a new feature — asking for user feedback at a certain point in the app. We spent a significant amount of time building it: collaborating with designers, we made an attractive and solid solution, something I was proud of. The end solution didn't look complex and had good test coverage (unit tests, integrations tests). In total, the work lasted for one month.

Now attention.

We had to cut-off 70% of the built functionality because the users found it too complex and didn't understand what the app wanted from them. Only a simple question "How was the experience?" with two options "I liked it" and "I didn't like it" remained.

And here's an example of fast prototyping with a positive connotation. The team was under time pressure and looking for ways to cut every minute of a new feature implementation. The user interface was supposed to be simple with little interactions but even that required a couple of engineering work days. My colleague Maria said something nobody could think of. She suggested putting the design mockup screenshot instead of implementing the page. The meeting room fell silent — we were processing what she said. It was genial: the idea saved an enormous amount of time. Since we planned to run multiple tests and iterate the page (we talk more about iterations in the following chapter), Maria's idea was 100% supported by the team.

Why would you build something you are unsure of? Opt for the simplest prototype instead.

Using a screenshot instead of actual design implementation went really well. The team ran the experiment and got results fast. We delivered within the deadline and did our learning.

I wish I had known it when we were building the feedback feature from the example above. If we had built a simple prototype in one week and launched it, we could have gathered the initial feedback and understood where to move. Instead, we wasted time polishing the code nobody used.

Agile & Iterations

This section is a logical continuation of the previous one. Thankfully, an overlap exists between the software engineering and product development worlds — where they agree that working in an agile environment brings most benefits.

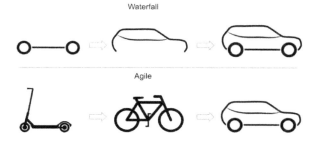

Comparison Waterfall vs. Agile methodology

The comparison above explains how agile works. In the first flow, we can enjoy the product only at the final stage. Meanwhile, in the second flow, we can use the product from stage I. Here we have a product that serves the user's needs — moving on wheels — from the very start.

The days of the Waterfall are gone. Agile methodologies are the common way of delivering projects. No matter what you stick to (Agile, Scrum, or Kanban), you still get many advantages compared to the Waterfall approach.

Why? The software industry has grown and understood that predicting if users will like and use your product is hard. Adapting it based on constant user research and feedback is safer.

This is about agile development, and iterations are at the base of it.

Each iteration should be short enough and bring some user value.

The crucial message for engineers is: don't worry about code, keep iterating. Firstly, you build an initial product. Next week you improve the code a bit and add more functionality. Next, you make the features even more solid and nicer. You come up with your "shiny" code in the end, only get ready to have a "working" environment for some time, don't be afraid of that.

For developers, a hard to swallow pill is the absence of an exact timeline for implementation and testing. They need to adapt quickly and accept that keeping the code clean is impossible.

Here's the main take-away: the value of the delivered product has a bigger impact than the shiny code. Once you accept it and learn to be more flexible, building new features and satisfying users gets easier.

I recommend reading the book *Scrum: The Art of Doing Twice the Work in Half the Time* by Jeff Sutherland. It explains the agile way of working, not only for software engineering. After reading the book you may start wondering why the entire world doesn't work that way yet.

User Testing

You can do user testing in many ways, starting as early as a prototype or mockups test. Sometimes it is fine to have a design only and ask user opinions. The feedback could be priceless.

As much as your team may be driven to build a great product they are biased and don't see the whole picture. Imagine building a product people would use in a completely different way. You are investing a lot of time in a new feature and your users don't need it.

"If your ladder is not leaning against the right wall, every step you take gets you to the wrong place faster". I like this quote by Stephen Covey as another confirmation for the need of user testing although he was writing about different things.

A while ago my team received a relatively trivial task. We had to build an application for runners. The standard user behavior would be: launch the app, press the "Start Run" button, press the "Finish" button when the run is over. Then you will see the screen with statistics: the distance, average pace, time, running path, etc. And while the person is using the app, a map with a distance and time should be visible. Nothing extraordinary, you've probably seen it in many other applications.

We did a proper planning split by features. It looked like a nice set of iterations. According to the plan, everything was supposed to be ready in three months. We were agile. We were prepared to adjust the plan in case of need but confident that we were building a cool thing. Our design looked impressive, we thought everybody would love it.

As a part of the releasing phases, we decided to make the product alpha version. It contained only core functionality but enough to use. We invited a few runners, gave them the devices, and talked to them after they had completed the runs.

At that moment we got the biggest insight.

The runners told us they were missing audio notifications such as an average pace. It turned out that the majority of runners use headphones and don't stare at their phones during the run. Duh!

And of course, if they are using a running app they wish to hear an update about their training from time to time.

That biggest insight forced us to update our roadmap. We shifted our focus to the audio announcements in the next iteration and built them immediately, without waiting for the final product. Only in a couple of weeks, we delivered that feature.

A user testing with only three athletes was enough to get that invaluable suggestion.

If three people complained about the same thing independently, you could trust it.

User testing is crucial to verify if the team is moving the right direction. Not sure if navigation on the website is clear? Do user testing! No confidence if using a carousel for selecting pictures is obvious? Do user testing!

Multiple tools will help you with it: special web resources (for example, *usertesting.com*), face-to-face interviews with real users, surveys.

Lastly, reliable user testing should be well prepared. Respect the time of others, don't make it long, maximum 20 min, usually it is enough for quality feedback. All the feedback is worth sharing and discussing it within the team. Everyone will appreciate it and will be eager to talk about it.

Who knows, maybe some of it will redesign your project roadmap for the better...

Collaboration

No matter how talented you are, synergies (and some great things) need a group of people to happen. Many researches prove: the way you work matters.

We have all heard and read about collaboration and how it is important for everyone. However, collaboration may vary: cooperation at an executives level is different from the collaboration between engineers.

In this section, we are going to explore how software developers can improve teamwork. Writing code and making it elegant is not our only value. In fact, being a team player with good cooperation skills may give a huge boost to your career.

Proactive Communication

I've seen developers acting as executors: give me a task and I will do it without questioning. This happens in some consultancy agencies when they live by the "Client is always right" rule. They merge into the code like robots and show up when the task is complete.

Is it something we want? Or would you prefer the developer to acknowledge problems if they exist, before they take more time and costs?

Treating the tasks mechanically is the wrong direction to follow. We want everybody to take initiative and speak loudly if things go wrong. Software engineers need to be involved in various product discussions in order to understand product needs. They should not sit quietly and wait for orders. Raising proper concerns about a feature complexity, asking questions about its capacity to solve certain problems, discussing potential improvements? — those are only a few proactive communication examples. Everybody will benefit from it. Product managers along with designers can understand the costs of adding that simple button to the product. And developers will plan a better application architecture according to future needs knowing the product intentions. Don't let silence suppress your growth. Remember, there are no stupid questions.

The topic of communication triggers in my brain many memories about successes and failures.

George Bernard Shaw said: "The single biggest problem in communication is the illusion that it has taken place".

In some cases, people don't get enough information and assume something instead. In other cases, they blindly trust their peers and don't ask follow-up questions. This is what exactly cost my team a month of clarifications.

We had to come up with a plan for the upcoming quarter. Our product manager James had worked in the field for 15 years, delivered to big names, and knew the process well. He had our complete trust. Every time he was presenting an intermediate proposal, we didn't scrutinize it. Because he simply could not be wrong.

Or could he?

Once he asked for our feedback before presenting the plan to the executive team.

We realized this was something we had to commit to and deliver.

I suddenly realized we'd been looking at the scope of tasks from completely different angles and I got seriously concerned if we could even deliver all of this. In the past, the best performing quarters had had a single clear goal. However, the proposal already contained three goals. My teammates kept silent but I felt the lack of confidence in the room.

So I raised my hand.

After I shared my concerns, more and more colleagues supported me. Did it upset James? No, he was actually happy to finally hear our honest feedback. We opened a few other rounds of discussions. Everybody realized it was safe to disagree.

In the end, we came up with a better proposal. The entire team was ready to commit. Together with James, we were able to make an impressive plan for the next quarter. Our success was measured by achieving several milestones. First, the executive team completely supported us and gave us a green light to implement it. Second, my team did proper research, designed and delivered a solid solution as it was planned. Third, based on metrics we increased application engagement by nearly 30%. All of this was possible only with the proactive involvement of each team member.

I have to admit though that for proactive communication, the environment has to be open to hear proposals and suggestions. Inappropriate jokes, irony, interruption are not acceptable. Everyone needs to respect each other and listen. Proactive communication brings great results when it is encouraged. Otherwise, it doesn't make any sense to constantly remind the team to share their thoughts and later criticize each of them, making them feel embarrassed.

Code Reviews

Code review is a great approach successfully adopted in the industry. The only prerequisite is that you need a teammate.

Code reviews help to look at your work results with a fresh pair of eyes and ensure you haven't forgotten to implement all functionality details. A reviewer can suggest another approach to build a feature and that can initiate a productive discussion within the engineering group. Reviewers can benefit from it, too. Once I discovered new things for myself while reviewing pull requests. It is a kind of knowledge sharing with your teammates.

If you haven't adopted code reviews practice in your team yet, then it is about time.

Once I joined a team where you could not integrate your piece of code without at least one approval of your teammate. My first impression was: "Oh, it will take ages to have my code live". I even remember arguing with my manager if we really needed it. Thankfully, he was calm and suggested giving it a try and later discuss the results. This was a right move as he also wanted to get an opinion from somebody new.

So I accepted the fact that shipping features became slower and I started trying.

During that time I made two important discoveries. First, the bigger changes you make, the more time code review takes. Therefore, code review teaches developers to implement atomic features. Software engineers are tempted to make some refactoring while implementing new functionality. But that will only slow down the review. It might sound that the changes of 500 lines of code are simple. When it is your turn to review the code, you will regret it.

Second, code review is a costly and limited resource. Nobody likes spending days checking your code and discovering missing tests or compilation errors. Developers will remain responsible for the changes they make as if they deliver them right to the customer. The reviewer should not be testing and fixing all issues. Instead, the reviewer is responsible for providing suggestions. For example, to use another function from the framework or apply best practices. The discussion can be started leading to a better final result.

After three months, I didn't have doubts about the code review's practicality.

Code reviews teach us to accept different opinions, ask proper questions. We analyze someone's work, provide constructive feedback instead of criticizing. It is widely adopted in open source projects where everyone shares responsibility. Software engineers put their best effort as they don't want to break code.

If you want to try code review practice, but your working environment doesn't allow it, pick up an open-source project. Either start your own or contribute to an existing one. You can also start with reviewing the code of other developers and giving them feedback. This experience will be full of insights.

Design Sprint

In one of the previous sections, we discussed iterations as an essential part of the Agile workflow. But they are not a single one. One of the greatest examples of Agile work is Design Sprint.

Design Sprint is an invention of Google. Its main goal is to understand a problem, explore potential solutions and build a prototype — all during one week. Jake Knapp's book *Sprint: How to Solve Big Problems and Test New Ideas in Just Five Days* explains in detail what should happen each day.

During the Design Sprint, the team should be 4 to 7 people with different professional backgrounds: marketing, design, engineering, management. And all of them are working on a single goal: figuring out how to solve a business problem. Don't confuse this with the Scrum Sprint despite both having Sprint in their name.

The result of the Design Sprint should be a testable prototype. It doesn't need to be a solution implemented with the code. Some of the successful prototypes were built with Apple Keynote or Microsoft PowerPoint. The team wants to get the validation of their idea with the least effort. During the Design Sprint, the team dedicates only one day to building a prototype itself. That's why it has to be done fast. The rest of the time is spent on brainstorming, ideas exploration, and making a decision.

What is more important, the Design Sprint teaches everybody to contribute to problem-solving. The team members are not solely engineers — on the contrary, the more professional diversity the better. People will try various approaches for achieving the goal.

Design Sprint is a simple process which addresses complex issues. Interestingly, taking a single isolated component — say one day from the sprint — is still ok if you have a time limit, however not very recommended. Stay open-minded and follow practices. Usually, after the Design Sprint, everybody gets a better understanding of the challenges the business faces.

Learning

Software developer's second nature is lifetime learning. Persistence to explore new technologies, understand how things work, and how to make them better. Sounds exciting as well as exhausting.

Some days you are just stuck on a problem for hours. This happens to senior engineers as well. What differs them, however, is how they tackle the problem. It relates to experience and no shortcuts exist.

Having said that, there is a way to speed up the process. You can improve your problem-solving skills and widen your horizons by doing the following activities on a regular basis.

T-Shaped Skills

Andrea has been working as a software engineer for the last 4 years and she is my good friend. Once I asked her about advice she would have given herself when she was only starting to work in the industry.

She answered. "I wish I had a single project in production for some period of time so that I could focus on mastering one technology. I was always changing projects and every project had a different technology stack. I've never felt confident."

Without thinking I replied that it was a great feeling — always learning and discovering new things. But there was a difference between us. I had twice as much experience as she. I didn't have to change projects as often as she did. Therefore, for me, her story looked like a great chance to explore some new frameworks. Then, in a few days, I actually understood her issue.

As a junior developer, you might feel overwhelmed due to the giant amount of information you get. It takes time and causes stress. You are trying to prove your worth. If the manager asks how much time it would take you to implement a specific feature, you are not feeling well in your stomach. How can you answer this question if you are seeing the framework for the first time in your life? Working a few months with that new framework is not enough to understand it, you will need more time.

Here we come to the necessity of dedicating a good amount of time to exploring specific technology. Both the employer and employee have to understand this investment. Although each person's learning process will differ in duration, it is integral for progressing in software development. And everyone will benefit from it: you as a software engineer, your team and your boss.

The story doesn't end here though. After you become an expert in a certain framework or technology, it is time to widen your horizons.

This is where the term T-Shape appears. Letter T consists of two pillars: vertical and horizontal. The vertical one means deep expertise in a specific field. The horizontal one stands for the broad horizons in other technologies. For example, if a person has excellent expertise in Ruby on Rails, then Node.js or React could be good candidates for further exploration. Honestly, that can be any field: frontend, mobile, data science. The idea is to apply the knowledge and experience in another area in order to achieve new heights.

How will you benefit from it? If the team builds a new feature, an engineer with a T-Shape skill set can understand the requirements and challenges in each piece of the solution. Backend engineers could understand better backward compatibility issues in REST API on the clients. For example, when a new version of the endpoint introduces new attributes in the response object. At the same time, mobile engineers will know the costs of each query and caching mechanism on a server. The collaboration between developers will increase. They will be able to exchange ideas and get necessary support.

In addition, it is a great career step for software developers. They will be able to contribute to multiple projects and become platform-independent specialists. Jumping between projects is usually not the best idea, but in case of urgency, it can resolve issues fast. Software developers with T-Shaped skills are good candidates for a management career. Having knowledge from every field enables taking into consideration all risks and making proper strategic decisions.

On a closing note, every engineer should strive for T-Shaped skills. And important is the order of achieving it: first is deep expertise in one technology, then shallow knowledge in other technologies. Otherwise, there is a risk that the person will never become an expert and will remain with shallow knowledge in every field. This will lead to poor performance and frustration due to the lack of mastery.

Reading Books

Mastering good coding requires a lot of practice. This is the only way to grow professionally. A smart approach though is to grasp the theory first and then apply it in practice. In the software development industry, it is a common thing to constantly educate yourself through reading articles, books, attending meetups, and trying out new libraries, patterns, and paradigms.

I have read many books to refine my programming skills, the list goes really long. The hand picked examples below can have alternatives but if you read them, you will be able to deliver readable and scalable code.

Algorithms by Robert Sedgewick

This book teaches basic algorithms such as search, sorting, and graphs. They are an essential part of computer science. This book will explain the implementation of the search functionality and the differences between sorting algorithms. One of the sections is dedicated to graph theory. After completing it, you will get the clarity on how to traverse a tree and find the shortest path.

Recognizing those algorithms and being able to apply them could be very helpful in your next job interview. An experienced software engineer knows in which situation to use an appropriate algorithm and what performance to expect.

In case you don't feel like reading a huge book and prefer listening to lectures instead, check a completely free course on *Coursera* from the book's author.

Code Complete by Steve McConnell

When I finished this book, I was surprised why nobody had explained such basic but crucial things to me until then.

What I mean goes next.

For instance, declaring and initializing a variable only in the place where it is going to be used. I discovered that declaring a variable and assigning it later somewhere in the code is considered a bad practice in programming. The variable should have the least visible scope possible. As the benefit, the code readability improves and your teammates will be thankful.

Another example is how to use *if* conditions efficiently. While learning programming, we focus on how the *if* condition works and when to use it — but nobody tells us how it could be misused.

Check the following example:

```
if (paymentComplete) {
  if (errorCode != 0) {
    ...
  } else if (errorCode == 422) {
    ...
  } else {
    if (showError) {
      ...
    } else { ... }
  }
} else { ... }
```

If conditions are simple but they can reduce code readability dramatically. The example above has too many nested *if* conditions, making it hard to follow and test the logic. The book gives advice: Avoid too many nested blocks, consider splitting the code into functions, and check if the *switch...case* statement is suitable (if the language supports it).

The book is worth reading for its practical examples — these and many others.

Functional Thinking by Neal Ford

Since the launch of functional programming in mid-20 century, its paradigm has been only getting more popular. This means the data are transformed through functions which can be composed into many levels.

However, it can be quite hard for junior developers to understand how to build stateless sequences. Even experienced developers who have never used functional programming may face challenges in writing efficient and maintainable functional code.

The following example in Kotlin does the summing of the squares of the even numbers:

```
val input = listOf(1, 2, 3, 4, 5, 6)
val result = input.filter { it % 2 == 0 }
                  .map { it * it }
                  .sum()
```

This can be done in a usual declarative way but that would require writing a few loops and saving intermediate states. Writing the code in a functional way makes it simpler, cleaner, and stateless. Apart from that, it is important to realize that the order of functions can play a big role in performance. Looking at the example, when the *filter()* method is called earlier, the following functions already operate on a smaller data set.

This book explains the most popular functions, teaches how to apply them efficiently, and how to write clean code in a functional way. It is recommended for developers who already have some coding experience.

***

With up-levelling skills over time, developers start looking for more and more technical challenges. As not all of them can tame their hunger, some jump between different companies.

However, changing jobs does not always lead to satisfaction. Challenging yourself through learning is a more practical way to keep growing as a professional. In this subsection, I will provide a list of technical books that every senior software engineer should read. They will encourage you to look at certain things from a different perspective.

Designing Data-Intensive Applications by Martin Kleppmann

This book is full of insight into how processing and storing data works. It covers database topics deeply. You will learn different types of databases and their most common use cases.

As developers, we know what database indexes and transactions are. But do we really know the cost of these features? How often do we question whether the performance keeps healthy with every newly added operation in a transaction? The author's answers to those questions are well-described on a bunch of real-world examples.

The author guides the readers not only through the databases, but also through the topics of data consistency and synchronization. For example, the mechanisms and approaches for achieving data consistency across distributed instances, when database replications are necessary, etc. You will learn about Atomic Commit and Two-Phase Locking in transactions when multiple writers are used.

This book is more useful for advanced engineers. It assumes you know the basics of computer science subjects, such as binary trees and hash tables. If you already have some experience in the field and want to better understand how big data systems work, this is a great starting point.

Design Patterns by the "Gang of Four"

After learning how to program and release multiple solutions, every developer starts observing some similarities in code. In certain cases, they would usually apply one approach. In other cases, a different common technique would be used. If you feel the same way, you have reached a turning point. Your next reading should be about design patterns.

A software design pattern is a technique for solving common problems in a conventional way. Instead of reinventing the wheel, we take advantage of well-known solutions and focus on business challenges instead .

The best book about design patterns is from the "Gang of Four" (Erich Gamma, Richard Helm, Ralph Johnson, and John Vlissides). It is famous among senior software developers and architects. It covers many design patterns, starting from simple ones like Singleton and finishing with more complex ones like Command and Visitor.

After reading this book, you may feel a little overwhelmed and tempted to apply complex design patterns to simple problems even when it is not needed. Use this book as learning material to expand your knowledge. Study all the examples they provide for every pattern.

With that said, next time you have to deliver a project, carefully pick the right pattern and strive for simplicity.

Java Concurrency in Practice by Brian Goetz

At first, we learn programming in a single thread — usually the UI thread. Things work well until we have to perform heavy computations or read/write files. The blocked user interface becomes a problem as it waits for the completion of the operation. That is the case when the job has to be done asynchronously and the user interface should remain responsive.

Even if your main specialization is not Java, this book can teach you about common problems in multi-threading systems. It starts by explaining what a thread is and how the system actually executes tasks in parallel. Then the book explains the most common problems with threads, like race conditions and deadlocks.

The book reminds us of the "dining philosophers problem" represented schematically below. Every person needs two forks to eat, therefore not everybody can eat at the same time. If some philosophers keep forks longer than others, you have so-called starvation. A situation of deadlock is also possible if every person takes only one fork. The problem highlights the equal usage of limited resources.

An example of "dining philosophers problem"

Later, the book dives deep into the topic of asynchronous task execution when the whole synchronization between parallel jobs is done by the framework.

The author focuses mainly on efficient parallel execution in the Java environment. Therefore, all examples are in Java. But you should not feel discouraged, as many other frameworks use similar ideas (e.g. .NET).

Concurrency is an advanced subject indeed. Start with this book when you feel confident in at least one programming language. After completing the book, you will have a clear picture of the costs of parallel work, non-blocking algorithms, and best practices in multi-threading systems.

***

As a software engineer, I sometimes feel like Alice in Wonderland listening to the Cheshire Cat. *"My dear, here we must run as fast as we can, just to stay in place. And if you wish to go anywhere you must run twice as fast as that"*, he said in Lewis Carroll's book. New technologies are continually appearing, and if we want to grow and build reliable solutions, we have to catch up with trends in the industry.

Staying curious is the key to succeeding.

Following Newsletters

A few ways exist for keeping up to date with your main technology stack. One of them is to subscribe to specialized newsletters, for example, Android Weekly to get the latest news from the Android world, This Week in Rails for Ruby on Rails recent updates, Python Weekly if you are curious about the Python world. Technology-oriented newsletters are a free source of knowledge. Engineers all around the world share their experience for free. You only have to take it.

Certifications

I have heard a few times that IT companies are not interested in certificates since knowledge and experience are more valuable than a piece of paper or a PDF file in that case.

However I will dare to root for certificates.

Recognized certification exams are proof for others that you study materials. A certificate might not guarantee you have practical experience but the knowledge itself is a good start to get that expertise. People know what kind of topics are covered in every certification program. They know that passing it is not a single day task. From this point of view, certification is valuable.

Some official certifications require a good level of preparation. You can't just come in and pass the exam. For example, exams for different Amazon Web Services (AWS) require refreshing knowledge even if you use those services every day.

Besides, preparing for an exam helps to understand the principles behind certain technologies. Think about NoSql databases. Do you know from the top of your head how indexing works there, and why picking up a proper sort key is crucial for performance? When we apply technologies in practice we don't always think about how things work behind the scenes. Only when we face issues, we start digging deeper and learn the details. Meanwhile, preparing for certification works the other way around. It is similar to the classic university course. First we learn theory, later we do hands-on.

Side Gigs

Something we can reveal after one or two beers with our teammates is that not every programming task is equally exciting. Yes, we love programming. But no, we are not robots. If we don't discover new things, add fuel to our learning fire, the urge to perform at our best capacity goes down.

Is there any quick fix?

Yes, starting a side project.

This sounds obvious, yet not many engineers do it. First, having a side project pushes you to think about the full lifecycle of it. You build a prototype, then you start thinking about having a good architecture. Then it comes to the deployment and project configuration, as we want to make sure that all parts are security compliant.

Have you ever had an idea of building something from scratch? Are you passionate about any technologies? Or maybe you want to try out a new approach? You can dedicate some time after work or on weekends. The reason it's called a side project is that you work on it only when you have time and pleasure. It is not a full time commitment.

Sometimes those projects can only run as an experiment and not go live. However, side projects can benefit you in many ways. It is knowledge and experience. In some cases you can learn a lot more from a side project than from a full time job. Because only you are in charge of how it will look like.

Different projects will require learning new skills. For example, suppose you decide to build an application for Android. You have to think well about UX and user flows. Building a good user interface is hard, and you may fail a couple of times unless you discover something suitable. When it comes to uploading the product to an app store, you will need to provide nice visuals, good descriptions, and a privacy policy. You will see it is not only about programming.

If you decide to build a project for the web, you will face other obstacles: where and how to deploy an application, selecting and configuring a database that satisfies needs, cost reduction of the running services.

I can't tell you how many times the knowledge I gained from side projects helped me to solve challenges at work.

But where do you start?

Picking up an exciting idea can be hard. Why not contribute to existing projects? I'm talking about open source. When you feel interested in an open source library, you can start contributing to it. You will learn how to read other people's code, get familiar with various design patterns, and receive some constructive feedback. You will learn how to collaborate with others and how to maintain a running project. You can't compare open source contributions to the business world, but you don't have to. It is a place where enthusiasts work on some topic they are passionate about in their free time for free. Their goal is not to earn money. Their goal is to build something for the community, something that will simplify life. This is an altruistic thing, but in terms of personal development it can bring a lot.

Side projects in the software industry are not solely programming. You learn to see the full picture of the application and to find the best suitable solution. Don't hesitate to jump in any topics. It will be rewarding in any case.

How to Learn Fast and Efficiently

Consistency Over Volume

When I was young, I enrolled in remote English classes. I was receiving all necessary materials along with assignments via post every month. The lessons and tasks were not numerous as learners were studying or working at the same time. When you looked at the tasks, you thought "I can do it fast, probably in 2-3 hours". A few hours a week is not that much, you can clean your schedule for that. This is what I was doing every Saturday.

However, the result was not as impressive as was promised. I didn't remember everything I learned. However, the advertisements kept showing "You need only 2 hours per week to learn English". So either something didn't work or I was doing it wrong. As I was reading more and more testimonials proving the course helped many people, I understood that it was me — I was not following the rules. I missed the main thing: the idea was to learn a bit every day and not to do a week's job on Saturday.

The only prerequisite for learning fast is consistency, even if it takes some time — ironically. If you adopt a daily routine, your learning will progress. It doesn't have to be hours. If we are talking about language learning, 20 minutes a day should be enough. Established habits are hard to break. Material repeated daily stays in long-term memory.

Speaking of programming, dedicate each day to solving programming challenges or read another chapter about how database internals look like. Small pieces of new knowledge will build a solid foundation for your future.

Schools successfully integrated this system by teaching students on a daily basis. Repeating materials and slowly adding new ones has been proven as a successful technique. If you learn something these days, find half an hour for it every day. In a few months, you will see astonishing results.

Write It Down

There are two reasons why students are asked to write lectures down. Firstly, so that later they can revise the material. Students take notes on the most valuable information. They organize received knowledge in a suitable format. Somebody will put down only a few sentences, someone else — a detailed abstract.

However, there is another reason why it is common to write down everything that your teacher says during the lesson. Think about it.

Especially these days, a teacher could simply print out all lessons and give them to students. Or even email everything. But that is not popular. Why?

Multiple research has shown that learning goes better through writing. More information remains in our heads if we take notes while listening compared to only listening. During writing our brain is actively working. It is difficult to write without thinking, but it's possible to listen without thinking. So when we write we force ourselves to think and to process the information we just heard. And this is how we remember it better.

Next time you watch a course about new technologies (for instance, Docker even though it is not that new), start taking notes. Write down with your own words how you understood it. Later in one week revise it. What are your feelings? The material will look familiar and you will be more confident handling it in your daily work.

No matter what you learn at the moment: studying for the university exam, preparing for some professional certification, or exploring business literature. It always makes sense to write down valuable information. It will help to remember more things in the long run.

Utilize Experience

With learning new things we acquire knowledge. With the knowledge application, we get experience. What should we do with experience? The right answer is to use it.

We can use experience for making work better and faster. But we can also use it for learning something new. Being familiar with certain technologies enables us to master new technologies. It widens our horizons so we can think in multiple directions.

For example, imagine you are a software developer coding in Java for the past 5 years. You feel confident enough with the programming language and various frameworks. For the majority of the feature requests, you already have a rough plan of what the implementation will look like. You are efficient and your solutions are resilient.

At someday, you have to learn C#, a programming language from Microsoft. The knowledge of Java will help on a new educational journey. Since you already know what polymorphism is and how garbage collection works, the learning curve will be gradual.

Sometimes we don't realize we can apply existing knowledge to get new knowledge.

It works well when we draw parallels and compare things.

A thirst for knowledge is natural for humans. Curiosity is our main driver to explore and discover new areas. Along with the proper methods for learning, we can come across many new things faster. And saved time could be used to get even more knowledge.

Knowledge Sharing

Once you reach some level of expertise in engineering, it's time to share it with the tribe. The principle "sharing is caring" is not only about food but also knowledge. Humanity has followed this principle for ages by transferring all achievements and learnings to the next generation. They already knew that this is a proper way to progress.

In this section we will go deep into all possible options on how to contribute to knowledge sharing. Because by giving something to others you get something back in return.

Local Meetups

A local meetup is a great place to start. Usually, in every big city, there are communities organized by interests. It can be Ruby on Rails community, .NET, Android, iOS, or around any other topic. People meet about once a month after work to hang out. Organizers take care of the venue and speakers so that you have some topics to learn about and later discuss with other participants. The atmosphere is friendly and you get to know people living in the same city. This can be beneficial when you start looking for a new job as established network connections can really speed up the process. Or you might help someone else to find it.

Don't underestimate the power of social connections and professional networks. We never know where life is taking us.

Another great opportunity is to start presenting at meetups. If you are new on the stage, unlike speaking at conferences, presenting at local meetups is not so challenging. The audience is small and open. Organizers are also happy to have you as a speaker because they give a chance to everybody and the competition is low. If you dream of improving your public speaking skills, this is your chance. After making a few presentations and addressing received feedback, you will notice how your confidence level rises. You will even develop your own style.

Your visibility as a software engineer starts growing and don't wonder if more recruiters will approach you.

There is always a big misunderstanding about the topics you want to present. Senior engineers keep thinking that there are no topics they can speak about. Many things look simple and obvious to them, and they assume they are not worth discussing.

This is a wrong assumption.

Something obvious to you might not be that obvious for others. Literally, there are no topics that any developer should not present. Take Git as an example. This everyday tool still has features that not everyone is aware of. Even those who know Git well will appreciate listening to your piece to refresh knowledge. Don't be afraid of judging, someone will always need your presentation.

Speaking at Conferences

After you start building confidence with presenting at meetups, try applying for various conferences.

Conference organizers select speakers based on their proposals. A proposal is a short text explaining what you are going to talk about and why participants should come to listen to you. Writing a good proposal is a skill that needs practicing — you need to know how to catch attention. Even experienced speakers with a good presentation track sometimes get rejected because their proposals didn't impress.

Once your proposal gets accepted it's time to make a good presentation. The key is to be prepared well. Define a logical structure for your talk, make a visually attractive presentation. Think about examples from your experience: the audience loves to hear real stories with takeaways. Make sure you do a dry run at least once in front of your colleagues to get some feedback.

One benefit of being a conference speaker is to have a lifetime recording and to overcome the fear of speaking in front of a big audience. This skill helps speaking proactively at work. In the end, everybody gets something out of it: the attendees learn something new, your employer is proud of having that outstanding developer and communicator and you keep growing professionally and personally.

Blogging

We spend a significant amount of time on becoming a better coder but we don't dedicate enough time to writing and communication. I know it is hard to imagine how those skills relate to software development. Yet, they determine your career growth.

Writing requires structuring and organizing thoughts. We talk here about writing technical documentation or technical articles for your company's blog. As an example, think about a recently delivered feature in past sprints. Now try to describe it in a couple of sentences in proper order. Describe it from the user's perspective: how it looks and what is the expected behavior. Then add technical implementation but in a way that is clear not only to your direct teammates but also to the CTO.

Many engineers would fail this task. They would attempt to rethink everything. After some time, they would present a newer version of the document. But it is still far away from good text. That proves that developers are usually not well prepared to explain things.

As a developer, I spend most of the time writing code and reading technical documentation. Unfortunately, mastering explaining skills is not a part of my daily duties.

These days the industry is changing and requires more and more involvement in building products. Since that type of work requires explaining technical details to non-technical coworkers, expressing minds clearly is a demanding skill. A good developer would behave as a mediator transforming technical details to the rest of the team. And writing as an activity can help a lot with that. Practicing it would deliver recognizable results over time. There are many opportunities to start writing: taking care of defining user stories, describing recent changes in the company's newsletter, gathering thoughts about the favorite open-source library in a personal blog.

"If you want to be a writer, you must do two things above all others: read a lot and write a lot." -Stephen King

To become a good writer, you have to write a lot. It means practicing more often is the key to success. But it is worth adding that it is not enough. A few things you can do to make your next technical blog post better.

Reading

Start reading more materials from other authors in your field. Through reading, we learn not only information, but also the structure of how it is written. Every author has their own style and targets their own audience. You will discover your own style at some point. If you don't have it yet, try experimenting — but reading is at the base of it.

As you understood from the chapter with recommended books, I dedicate a lot of time to reading. Some big part of my career development and readership growth have become possible thanks to this activity.

Feedback

Don't be afraid to ask for feedback. Constructive feedback about your blogs from your colleagues or friends can help you to look at them from a different angle. Try to understand the reasons behind every feedback you get. It doesn't mean you have to address all of them but it is worth doing some analysis and to learn from it.

Giving feedback has to be a dialog. Both parties exchange their opinions, share feelings and look for improvements. Receiving feedback is just as challenging as giving it. When we provide feedback, we have to evaluate the person's work from an independent point of view and stay unbiased. While receiving feedback, we need to realize that it is neither a criticism or praise. We take it into account and adjust our behavior. Probably the best way to understand how feedback should be is to recall the quote of Frank A. Clark: "Criticism, like rain, should be gentle enough to nourish a man's growth without destroying his roots."

Audience

Before you start writing, consider your target audience. Writing about fashion or lifestyle is different from writing about technology. Writing for your team is different from writing for your boss. The content can't be delivered in the same way.

Next, if an article is a technical "How to" tutorial, you should take into account the audience experience. Beginners are excited about learning something new, but experienced engineers might not be impressed. Ask yourself for whom exactly you are writing it. Making everyone happy is impossible, try to focus on your target group, and create the best content for them.

Workshops

I once attended a workshop by my colleague, James. He was very passionate about reactive programming and tried to apply it anywhere possible. Meanwhile, I was not a big fan of it and thought reactive programming had to be used carefully and only in specific situations.

James' presentation was about using reactive programming in a new framework. At the end of the presentation, I understood what kind of problem he tried to solve by applying that new framework. It opened my mind to state management issues (stateful versus stateless) that I had never considered seriously. It was an opportunity to widen my horizons in programming and stateless applications. The discussion after the presentation was even more interesting as we had engineers with different backgrounds. On certain platforms like .NET and Java, reactive approaches are used extensively, in languages like Python and Ruby they are not common. Every developer learned new things.

Consider organizing a knowledge-sharing workshop for your teammates. It doesn't have to be a high-profile presentation but rather a hands-on case. For inspiration, you can explain how to write good unit and integration tests or explain complex architectural patterns.

If you do this on a regular basis, you will see astonishing results. Your teammates will be curious to listen about technologies, best practices, or new approaches. Don't get discouraged if some of them don't appreciate it or disagree — this may start an interesting discussion with the involvement of the entire team. During those conversations, you might come up with new conclusions and ideas. Don't be frustrated if you don't get only positive feedback. Constructive feedback helps to understand better how to organize a talk next time and what the team is curious to learn about. Also, don't limit the presentation only to already applied technologies: it is always good to get a breath of fresh air.

Although a workshop for your team is not as demanding as a conference presentation, it also requires preparation. Your colleagues will treat you as a topic expert so spend a few hours preparing for it. You have to adjust your talk depending on the audience. Presenting iOS-specific topics for iOS developers is exciting for them and they would love to see some pieces of Swift code. Presenting it to Javascript people won't be as much appreciated. We need to pick examples that are clear for everyone. If the talk is about a new approach (like reactive programming in James' case), it is enough to have diagrams and pseudocode. This will be more informative than the code in a specific language.

Once you make this workshop a few times and address received feedback, it can become a conference talk or a workshop for a wider audience like one at a local meetup.

Content Production

If you are working for a small company, knowledge sharing can be challenging. This should not stop you: if you have interesting ideas, the world needs to know about them.

Thankfully, the digital era makes finding your audience possible.

Have you ever thought of making an online course? Although we can assume that we have average skills and nothing interesting to teach, in most cases it is not true. We have years of experience in a certain field with certain technologies, and beginners want to suck every piece of information. This is a great opportunity to step in. E-learning keeps growing every year as more and more people are willing to improve their skills from the comfort of their homes.

Start from picking your niche.

My colleague Michael launched a YouTube channel about iOS development. In German.

I was surprised. I asked him if he was sure about it because English-speaking audience was much wider in the software development industry. So if he wanted to grow his audience, I thought, he needed to target a larger number of potential followers.

His answer impressed me.

He said: "I want to tell more about the iOS platform to German students. At the beginning of their career, they are not proficient in technical English. They prefer to search for learning materials in German. There are not enough articles, videos in German".

With time, students and junior developers will improve their English but at the start of their career, mastering English can be overwhelming. When I got my first job in an old brick office, to solve technical tasks, I was searching for information only in Russian. Only later, as my proficiency in programming grew, I started looking for guidance in English as it was the only option.

Now I was not surprised that Michael's YouTube channel in German turned successful. With consistent releasing of new videos, he managed to get 10 000 subscribers in only one year, and it keeps growing.

No matter how many video courses exist, you can still find your niche. Split the audience of engineers into smaller groups: junior developers, experts, speaking different languages, coming from other professions, focusing only on a very specific topic like Collections in Java.

If videos is not your type of content, you can consider starting a podcast. The industry of podcasts is booming and mostly because of its format. It is easy to produce it compared to videos and easy to consume it for instance, during shopping or cleaning the house. Pick up a topic, prepare the script, and record it. You can start small with 10 to 15 minutes episodes explaining how some technologies work or best practices in software development. Later you can evaluate if you like podcasting and what people think about it.

To continue inspiring you, here is another potential area — becoming an instructor or coach. Some people prefer learning not from recorded videos but from direct interaction with a teacher. We can utilize this opportunity and organize classes in the evenings or at weekends. A small group of students would be the most efficient in terms of a personal approach. This can be a one-time event or a series on a certain topic. For example, there was an event from the Ruby Girls group in Munich a couple of years ago. They organized a workshop on a weekend to quickly explain how the Ruby on Rails framework works and to teach building web applications. Why not do something similar?

An alternative is to host a webinar. In this case, you don't need to worry about the location and organization process. You would focus solely on delivering materials.

Project management

Sooner or later every software engineer has to deal with project management. This doesn't necessarily mean becoming a project manager — rather understanding the project's lifecycle. Planning, estimations, testing, communication with stakeholders are only a few activities every project manager performs. And to serve your team better, developers need to understand its principles and duties.

Estimations

Estimations are hard. Every developer struggles with this task. The reason is simple: developers are asked to estimate something they haven't done yet. (Unless it is an agency delivering white-label apps with exact same functionality).

With experience, estimations get more precise but the uncertainty doesn't go away completely. Yet how can you succeed in it?

Estimate by hours

Once I worked for a company where we had quite strict rules regarding estimations and time tracking. For every new feature request we got, we had to estimate it precisely. There was a rule: the task could not be shorter than 15 minutes as it didn't make any sense to spend less time performing it than reporting about your work. And the task could not be longer than 2 hours. When it was longer, we had to split it into subtasks.

All of it may sound like an overhead and cause pressure. On the other hand, it teaches discipline and responsibility. Nobody was telling me sign-in functionality takes 2 hours. Handling that kind of answer was easy. Try to explain to the developer that all work beyond an estimate will not be paid. It doesn't have to happen, but at least engineers take responsible action while doing their next estimate. We all know how it usually happens: we forget a few tiny details and the feature is already 4 hours to complete, twice the initial estimation.

Advice: take some time to decompose every feature request in advance. Think about every possible use case including error handling. Is there an error dialog if the network call fails? Can the user retry?

Estimate by days

Another possible way to perform estimations is to round them to full days. For example, implement the registration feature — two days, implement the sign-in feature — one day. Compared to the first way of estimations, this type causes less time pressure, but increases the project's costs. If you don't feel confident with your estimation skills, consider this option as a compromise for the budget.

Besides, estimating by days gives a time buffer if something is missing. For example, if you planned to spend 2 days to complete the registration feature, it feels less stressful compared to delivering it in 14 hours. You can take time to do a proper architecture design, add necessary tests and make sure nothing got forgotten. This approach gives a chance to cover all possible scenarios while building a feature.

There will be tasks that would take an hour to complete. These and similar tasks need to be combined so that we could tell we need one day to complete 3 tasks.

Advice: think about each task as a complete and independent feature. Then try to evaluate how many 8-hours days you would need to complete it. Is one day enough? Why do you need three days and not two? Don't hesitate to add some buffer.

Don't estimate at all

Once I joined a team under the leadership of a professional scrum master. He'd already had years of experience dealing with processes and applying the latest agile methodologies. What surprised me was that his team didn't estimate. No days, no story points, no T-shirt sizes. Nothing. My first question was "how does this team complete every sprint on time without estimations?".

A discussion with him gave me valuable insight. Every second Monday the team did sprint planning. They defined what they wanted to accomplish in the next sprint. The stories in the backlog were prioritized by the product owner in advance. So the team took a few of them from the top of the backlog.

Who controlled how many stories to take? The scrum master. He analyzed statistics from every sprint and saw that most stories were the same size. Each story took on average 3 days to complete and in a 2-weeks sprint, the team was able to deliver 3 stories. To understand the system better, I would recommend to listen to the lecture #NoEstimates from Allen Holub.

In this case, the team didn't know anything about estimations. The scrum master controlled the size of each story and whenever it seemed too big, he split it into smaller stories based on the discussion with the product owner.

Advice: If the team struggles with estimations, suggest counting stories to complete.

Find a person to delegate evaluating the amount of work to do, but not estimating.

***

Estimations are hard. Nobody likes doing estimations because it is a commitment to something we are not sure about. More precise estimation comes through practice. Also to learn from missed deadlines — this is a cruel teacher which makes your next estimates more accurate.

Problem-solving

Is it possible to assess problem-solving skills? I've been thinking about it a few times and couldn't find the answer.

While testing for problem-solving, some companies give a technical test. For example, different modifications of the search algorithm or graph related questions. Although to me, they test technical knowledge and don't reach the real skill of solving issues.

However, when you see great problem-solving skills, you know it on the spot.

Once we had a project for retail shops. There was nothing unique: regular UI, authorizing different users, listing selling items. We also had to arrange printing receipts. It could have been a trivial task if the printer had had an SDK.

The absence of an SDK turned into a colossal problem. Researching online didn't help. The vendor suggested buying their newer (read more expensive) printer model which had an SDK. We were devastated. Without the receipt, the entire solution was useless. Buying a newer printer was not an option as the competition was tough and the budget limited. I felt stuck like never before.

At that time, I had an intern in my team. His name was Eduardo, and he was a third-year student at a local university. He was very curious and enjoyed working on something real compared to the university. We decided to delegate the printer issue to him as I needed to give my mind a break because this lousy printer was driving me crazy and I couldn't concentrate on anything else.

The next day Eduardo told me he had a working solution.

A working what?

He proposed to write necessary data to a file and then a system service would watch that file and send it to the printer directly if any changes take place. This was mind-blowing. After many years, I still remember our conversations and the technical details. Eduardo didn't focus on finding an SDK or connecting to the printer through the app. He focused on a problem: how to print text. This was the main difference between Eduardo's approach and mine.

An outstanding developer must have the ability to spot a problem and solve it. They also shouldn't be afraid to make dents in shiny code: those things can be addressed later.

Questions about problem-solving skills often come up during job interviews. The question usually sounds like 'What was the biggest challenge you faced at work and how did you solve it?'. Eduardo definitely has something to describe.

Technical Documentation

A lot is said about the importance of technical documentation. Software engineers encourage everyone to have good documentation on the product and applied technologies.

Yet, it's not as good as everybody wants it to be. Often, it doesn't cover all scenarios and leads to even more confusion. Sometimes the documentation exists, but it describes not what developers are looking for but the exact opposite.

We have to understand that a single shared document is usually not enough to be called technical documentation. Let's find out what kinds of documentation exist and how to maximize their benefits for your team.

API Contracts

The first thing that many engineers think of when they hear the word "documentation" is API documentation. This is what software developers use almost every day. API documentation refers to the description of classes and methods in frameworks and libraries. The REST API is another example that's expected to have well-formulated documentation.

Now, ask yourself how often you write documentation for the cases mentioned above. Do you write what each class does in the comments? Do all your REST methods have a place where all possible responses are defined? And, importantly, do you need to do it?

To answer these questions we need to know who the product's end-user is. If we're building a framework, our users will be engineers. If they want to use it in the most effective way, they should know how to do that. So, all public classes and methods must have complete documentation. A good example is *JavaDoc*, where the final documentation can be generated out of comments. Every platform has its own subsidiary service to deal with documentation.

It's exactly the same with the REST API. For public use scenarios, software developers have to implement clients that are able to use it efficiently. They need to know mandatory headers, parameters, how to authenticate users, and sign each request. A lack of this information complicates the final product usage.

How different is the process when the product is not a technical tool for other programmers — for example when the team is building an application for ordering taxis? There are no public classes or API to share with the rest of the world, so does it make sense to document everything?

There are many opinions on this topic between two extremes: some say the code should be self-explanatory, others — that the code always remains in a private repository, only for internal use, and therefore, doesn't need documentation.

We can agree that well-written code doesn't require documentation — it should be clear how to use it. When the code is not straightforward, we might need to make a comment on how it's being used and why.

The code and API in such products are permanently changing as the product adapts to the market needs. What is the reason to write documentation to the class that becomes legacy already in 6 months? While that is true for classes, it is not really applicable to the REST API as it usually lives longer. Even when it is clear to the team, within a year newcomers will ask how certain endpoints work and what the response format is.

As not everybody is capable of answering those questions, documenting them will help to disseminate knowledge outside the team. This is an investment for the entire company that will remind the team how API works, help other teams to contribute to that field, and help newcomers to catch up more quickly.

Approaches and Flows

Apart from API documentation, there's more to paperwork: describing how various components interconnect and communicate with each other. This is a great example of how to utilize API documentation of a third-party service and to adapt it to the product needs.

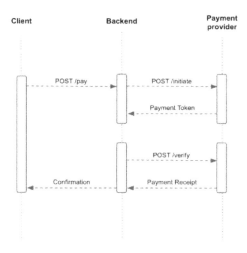

Example of flow/approach documentation

The schema above represents a classic example of flow documentation. It shows how to initiate a payment request from the client to the backend with an integration of the payment provider. We can see there are multiple components: client, backend, payment provider. Each of those components is independent but useless without the integration with the rest.

Documenting the approach or flow helps you to design the final product. It enables sharing the understanding within the team of how the entire system works — for instance, how the whole payment system works. Otherwise, some important details, like why payment verification is mandatory, could be missing or wrongly interpreted.

Designing this kind of documentation is harder. It requires knowledge of the business area and a technical part. The person preparing the document must have good analytical skills with an ability to decompose the whole into pieces. It's necessary to express everything in a clear and understandable manner. Think of it as a document that will be read by thousands, even if it is intended only for a team of ten. This documentation is going to live longer than the API of some classes.

Mastering the skill of writing good documentation helps to achieve a new level in career growth. Because it covers all areas of the final solution and demonstrates the architectural vision, it can be referred to at any time. That makes this kind of documentation really valuable.

Writing documentation is not as exciting as writing code. However, this makes you collaborate with others. Big solutions involve more engineers and even more communication. The best communication tool for a software developer is technical documentation.

There are plenty of instruments available for implementing and maintaining documentation. No matter which one you choose, the goal is to have documentation. Start now and you will never regret it.

Leadership

After spending years in the software development industry and gaining solid experience, engineers need to pass their knowledge on to the next generation. When you have theoretical and practical experience, it's time to guide others — but only when you've mastered both. With that combination, learning blossoms.

If you feel like you have something big to share but also want to take on the next big challenge, go through the following opportunities. They will take you to a new level and can fulfill your aspirations.

However, keep in mind: these opportunities do not relate to programming directly. You will do less actual coding. This is a trade-off you have to deal with. If you want to gain new experience, you have to sacrifice something.

Become a Mentor

In your team, you probably have people with different levels of expertise: interns, trainees, junior engineers, senior engineers, principals. They have something in common: passion about technologies and programming.

But not all of them have enough experience.

This is an excellent place to step in as a mentor. As a knowledgeable colleague, you can bring more value than simply coding.

Think about it as a task only you can solve. And the task is company performance.

When you share your skills with colleagues, the company performance increases. Firstly, you will not be alone to resolve specific issues. Although some might think that having a unique skill is a way to ensure your job security, it doesn't benefit you in the long run. Also, think about the situation when you are striving to explore a new technology and need some help. Would you like to have a colleague that does not want to share and explain information? Most likely, no.

Secondly, your colleagues will be grateful. They will appreciate any valuable feedback from your side, for example, reviewing pull requests and suggesting ideas to do things differently.

Do you remember how my career as a software engineer started — in an old red brick building where a small IT firm was based and I was overwhelmed with information? I suffered through my first weeks at work — so much I had to learn, but my sufferings could have been much worse if not for my mentor, Andrew. I was so lucky I had him! Andrew was both smart and experienced, and my life in the office was so simpler under his guidance.

Out of my gratitude and desire to give back, later I would often step up as a mentor to newcomers. Admittedly, it wasn't always easy as the mentor and mentee were not on the same page. The experience gap didn't let me explain things how I wanted to say them and I had to think much deeper and try to rephrase it so that I myself — minus ten years experience — could understand it.

However, mentorship gave new depth to my own knowledge, too. We used to have a joke that 'I was explaining it so many times I finally understood it myself'. In search of the best possible explanation of some technical details to my mentees, I had to scrutinize our work in such minuscule fragments I would have never done solely for myself. My expertise as a software engineer gained volume. And on top, I learned to find proper words to explain anything to anyone. Seriously.

Albert Einstein once said: "If you can't explain it simply, you don't understand it well enough". Becoming a mentor is a great opportunity to learn how to explain the material. And while explaining it you might discover more and more unclear points.

So it can turn into mastering certain topics.

Technical Coordination

Another opportunity on your way to leading others is to become a technical coordinator. Many companies have invented different names for this role: team lead, tech lead, engineering manager. No matter the name, the responsibilities are similar. If your team doesn't have a person in a similar role, you can use this chance to take it over. What do you need for it?

Good team leads are usually grown within the company and get promoted to this position.

Firstly, someone with a leadership role is expected to know the details of the running business, and on top of it — to have a full picture of the application you are working on.

As a team lead, you will program less and less. Your teammates will expect you to act as a coordinator. The role of technical leadership is to delegate task execution. While the team is implementing a new feature, you have to make sure they make the right decisions. You have a clear overview of the product development and your guidance helps to deliver scalable and reliable solutions. The expertise you own becomes the source of truth.

Secondly, a technical coordinator must communicate well. You should get rid of information silos. All necessary information has to be shared with everyone in the team and in a timely manner. Overcommunicaing and repeating the same things is better than refraining from bothering people. This creates better awareness. Meanwhile, poor communication generates mistrust, gossiping, and false expectations.

Being a coordinator requires understanding all business processes — from marketing to customer support. Analyzing the business status quo, and supporting it or suggesting changes will bring even more value to you as an expert.

Team Spirit

A good team doesn't materialize from nothing. It is the work and contribution of each member. However, some initial drive is needed. When people feel they belong to a certain group, they get involved. They want to do their job better, as it is visible within the team.

This is a moment when you can take initiative. You can organize a team event. The best example of this is an internal hackathon. Engineers like to explore new technologies and switch their minds away from their daily routines. A hackathon can be only a few hours long and dedicated to a specific topic. There is no reason to go crazy and keep coding for the whole weekend. Even with a mini format, ideas from developers will start popping up.

Align with the manager about ordering food and drinks and reserving some time. Business owners will be happy to give this chance to the team, as new revolutionary ideas can come up.

As an event organizer, you will spend a good portion of your time on communication and planning. It is a good opportunity to learn how to bring people together to reach goals and keep them involved. Be ready, this will take a lot of energy.

I organized three internal hackathons in different companies. My first hackathon was a mess.

Initially, I thought it would require almost zero work. That was a mistake. I needed to prepare the venue and the schedule, bring some paper, markers, define the format for the pitches and guide the participants. This already gave enough stress but the most challenging part was to encourage people to share their ideas and form teams. You can't just say "Now, go and do some hacking", a lot more effort and creativity is required from the organiser to help the participants do some magic and enjoy the process.

Along with planning the hackathon kick off, you need to think about the final presentation. The teams would need all opportunities to show the results. I had to figure out how to connect to the beamer on the go. Because I didn't explain properly how to use the hardware, one team spent 3 out of 5 minutes of their presentation trying to solve the connectivity issue. I felt very guilty.

When the hackathon was over, I analyzed my mistakes and did better the next time. I also understood how to approach different people because the same methods do not work for everyone.

Building trustful relationships takes a lot of time, and a single team activity is not enough. Bringing people together on a regular basis assists in establishing a team spirit, by managing teams and events you will develop the skills which are in high demand these days.

***

If you feel the technologies in your field can no longer satisfy your hunger, it is still possible to find growth opportunities. Look around to see if any of your colleagues need help or if processes in the organization can be better. It all depends on your perspective.

There are plenty of career opportunities to pick up. Start acting on them!

Conclusion

Growing professionally, climbing a career ladder is a task that requires commitment, dedication and perseverance. You need years to become a professional, and it's true for any field. Teachers, lawyers, doctors require time investment before they can solve complex and challenging tasks. The same applies to the software development industry.

We put time into learning and exchange it later for experience. We trade it to have an ability to solve problems quickly. We are interested in putting in the least amount of time to get the same output. This book combines my many years experience as a software engineer. My intent was to save your time. This book should guide you through the career path and bring insights. The opinions and observations in this book are not only mine but also shared by my colleagues and friends. Many of them, including me, were looking for similar advice in a professional life. However, take this book with a grain of salt as the differences in cultures and companies might have an impact on your goals and ways of working. There are no answers to all questions. But it is in our capacity to find the missing ones and tell others.

I believe sharing all my experience and knowledge with you makes the software industry a bit better. Therefore I'd like to ask you, the reader of this book, to share your opinion with me. What do you think is missing? What needs to be included? What needs rework? I promise to use your feedback for the next edition.

Also, if you believe your colleagues may learn something interesting in this book, please share it with them.

Recommended Resources

These are the books and other resources recommended by the author:

Design Patterns by the "Gang of Four"

Start With Why by Simon Sinek

The Design of Everyday Things by Don Norman.

Scrum: The Art of Doing Twice the Work in Half the Time by Jeff Sutherland

Sprint: How to Solve Big Problems and Test New Ideas in Just Five Days by Jake Knapp

Algorithms by Robert Sedgewick

Code Complete by Steve McConnell

Functional Thinking by Neal Ford

Designing Data-Intensive Applications by Martin Kleppmann *Java Concurrency in Practice* by Brian Goetz

Video lecture *#NoEstimates* by Allen Holub Official Git tutorial: git-scm.com

Design patterns mentioned in the book: Observer, Factory, Singleton, Facade

To improve your programming skills, visit: hackerrank.com, leetcode.com

Tools for tracking: firebase.google.com, mixpanel.com

A tool for user testing: usertesting.com.